T0063114

framed in faith

in

faith

A journey in trust

Melinda Laird

WestBow
PRESS
A DIVISION OF THOMAS NELSON
& ZONDERVAN

WestBow Press books may be ordered through
booksellers or by contacting:

WestBow Press
A Division of Thomas Nelson & Zondervan
1663 Liberty Drive
Bloomington, IN 47403
www.westbowpress.com
1 (866) 928-1240

ISBN: 978-1-4908-4695-8 (sc)
ISBN: 978-1-4908-5014-6 (e)

Library of Congress Control Number: 2014913723

Printed in the United States of America.

WestBow Press rev. date: 8/27/2014

There are times in our life when things happen that we never thought possible. The time will devastate us, change our life and knock us down. It is through the healing that we see the relationship that God has called us to have with Him. This will make us stronger.

"I can do all things through him who strengthens me." Philippians 4:13 (ESV)

Mike and Makila, this is for you!

Acknowledgements

There are many many people for me to thank and acknowledge who have been with me along my journey. I have been richly blessed by girlfriends from Oklahoma to North Carolina and those in between who have been in prayer for me during this period of trial and tribulation. When I began to write I enlisted some help as my "writing angels." I want to thank Ginger, Hope, Debbie, Cathy, Cary and Alice for their eyes and hearts to give me their thoughts and correct my typos, love them all! Melissa, there is no way I would have stayed on course without your encouragement and editorial guidance. I love you sister!!! Alice, what a mighty prayer warrior you are, your prayers have been felt across the country. Thank you for your walking prayers!!

Family, I love my family. The family I grew up with and the family I married into with Mike. My parents love me and have provided me with a great foundation. I have two wonderful brothers who have married wonderful women I now call sisters.

Mike is someone that I am so glad God placed us together on this journey; He knew what He was doing when He put us together. You have challenged me, encouraged me and always love me. We have a beautiful daughter that God blessed us with and I thank Him so much for allowing us to have her and what she has brought to our lives.

To the women who will read this book, thank you. There are many of us that are in stressful careers, trying to balance the career with our family, and this leaves us drained and questioning God. I have been on a career path that has a high turnover rate and leaving me questioning my career. Ladies, you are not alone, ever. God is with you and wants to have a close intimate relationship with you. It is the *only Way* for us to get through our life.

Contents

"Make a joyful shout to the Lord, all you lands!

Serve the Lord with gladness; Come
before His presence with singing.

Know that the Lord, He is God;

It is He who has made us, and not we ourselves.

We are His people and the sheep of His pasture.

Enter into His gates with thanksgiving,
And into His courts with praise.

Be thankful to Him, and bless His name.

For the Lord is good; His mercy is everlasting,

And his truth endures to all generations."

Psalm 100 (NKJV)

Introduction

We are all on a journey growing in our relationship with Jesus Christ, our Lord and Savior. When I began writing this message it was to be all about trusting God in the decisions in our life. Sounds simple, right? It grew to be so much more than that one message. It's just like God to take you further than you ever imagined. This message grew to be about a relationship of faith that is about trust and obedience to God. It is a message that reveals the faithfulness of God in our life. This at times seemingly faithless world, He is faithful.

I wonder how many of us are so involved with our life, with our church that we miss the real relationship. It's not that you know church; it's not making sure your children know church; it's not how many times you are at church or being the model church lady. It is the relationship with Jesus Christ, the relationship for you and the relationship for your family. This is a relationship that has trust like you have never known in your life and can't imagine.

I was raised in a Christian home. Growing up we went to church and Sunday school most every Sunday. I attended youth group and church camp. I remember the day I accepted Jesus Christ as my Savior, my mother cried and we celebrated. Faith was part of my life. This is the experience in my life that brought me closer to Christ. Faith needs to grow for each of us. That's where it can get uncomfortable for us. The trials and storms we go through in life are different and praise God He loves each one of us the same and grows each of us differently. We are on a journey of growth and change similar to the changing of seasons. A growth that brings us to grab hold of the relationship with Jesus Christ, to stretch. I am sharing with you a part of my journey, my changing season that was a humbling and powerful experience for me and for my family. It is not a job, a church, or a status in a profession or a community that is to be the priority in our life. This was a time when I learned to lay my every day burdens at the cross and learned the powerfulness of "being still in His presence." Above all I learned what is important in my life, the love of our heavenly Father and my relationship with Him.

This message has been placed on my heart to share with you and I thank God. This is a place where God woke me, shook me and I began to grow in my relationship with Him.

I'm not a writer. Never in my wildest dream, was writing a book something that I thought I would do in my life. My high school English teacher has to be smiling up there with God because I definitely remember her frown when reading my senior writings. Then there was grad school, I enlisted help to get me through, just for writing.

As one of my BFF's likes to say, "*But God,,,*" always has another plan. His plan for our life is definitely different and always better for us. We are to be ready to be obedient and to trust Him.

The book can be read on your own or in a small group. Each chapter will have 3-4 responses for you to reflect and answer in your own thoughts or share with others. The best revelations we have are when we have that special friend or group of friends to share and grow together.

There are many people who have grown me and taught me the glory of friendship. Just like the story of Job's friends, Eliphaz, Bildad and Zophar who came to be with him and comfort him during his troubles, I have learned what that kind of friendship can mean in my life. Friends from Oklahoma to North Carolina back to Oklahoma are a part of this message. There are two that I want to share with you. Melissa in Oklahoma listened to God and called me. She listened and then turned me back to faith. Ginger in North Carolina listened to God and showed up. She would just appear at our house sometimes late at night, just because I gave to short of a text response. Both of these women I love with all my heart and taught me how deep the love Father God has for us.

My prayer in writing this has been for women in any and all walks of life to see passion and joy in having a relationship, a deeper relationship with God. We have challenges and trials in every phase of our life. Women are in leadership positions, running businesses, working, supporting families, homeschooling, just to name a few and it is in these roles that we learn to trust God. Learn to grow in our faith and listen to His word, His voice and Love. The hope we have to not let the trials and burdens overtake us because we have our hope in Jesus Christ. That hope is available to all of us because of who we call Friend, Jesus Christ and what He did for all of us.

God takes you where you never thought you would be going.

Getting My Attention

Trust is a simple word with only 5 letters that can put fear, anxiety and even anger in us. Why do we fear this commitment? There are signs and messages all over that say "trust us". They are saying things like: "you can trust us we do good work"; "you can trust us with your car"; "you can trust us with your care"; "you can trust us with (you fill in the blank) " _____", and on and on and on. How easy can that trust be torn down in our world. Relationships have been broken, families torn apart and friendships lost due to misplaced trust. For many of us trust does not come easy or without a cost, it's difficult for us to trust anyone once we have that callus that tough skin built over our brokenness. Even in our relationship with God we say we trust Him, but we make sure that we control the situation or definitely we control the outcome. Our relationship with God is ever present in our lives more one sided from Him as we come and go, we take ourselves out of the relationship. **There is nothing**, nothing that we can do that He will ever leave us to never return. Do we test that trust? Absolutely, we've been burned in this humanness. We want to make sure of the direction of God because when we asked and it didn't have the outcome **we** expect, it takes too long, or it isn't what we wanted to happen, we question. We test. You know the list; if you've not said it out loud, it's been in your heart.

So what does it mean to trust God fully, completely, without question? Trust God with everything in my life, every circumstance and every area of my life? Really?? In everything? All?

Proverbs tells us to "trust the Lord with all our heart." Psalms tells us several times, as does the New Testament, to trust. There are approximately 40 verses about trust and trusting in the Bible. To go further, we look at our relationship with God, as we have had trust issues with individuals it has impacted our relationship with God. Where is our relationship with God? We go about the business of honoring God in what we do and think that is trusting God, when we should be giving Him the glory and living our lives for Him, in everything. We are to shift the perspective from our humanness to His holiness.

In 2008 my faith journey took a turn that led me to learn what it means to always, always, always be about Him. Depending on God, having a meaningful relationship with God, brings a joy to us that far exceeds our humanness. We are on a journey and there is JOY on this journey that is amazing for us, we just have to trust.

Here is my story of understanding how to truly trust God and deepen my relationship with Him.

> *...,I remind you to fan into flame the gift of God, which is in you through the laying on of my hands. For God did not give us a spirit of timidity, but a spirit of power, of love and of self-discipline.*
> 2 Timothy 1:6-7 (NIV)

I'll start in 2008, because up until then I really had what I thought was a pretty good life. I'm a good person. I am married to a wonderful man who shares in this journey with God. God has truly blessed our marriage with a beautiful daughter, after many childless years and frustration of infertility (but that's another story!); she is such a joy in our lives.

Then in July 2008, my comfortable happy good life was turned completely upside down.

One night in a hotel room in Omaha, Nebraska I was on my knees crying out to God, "Why", "What have I done?" "Why?" "Why?"...

A trip that I thought was to be a strategic planning offering for leadership instead became a time to tell me that I would not be part of the new leadership of the organization where I had committed the past 7 years of my career. The CEO that I had as a mentor and learned a great deal from was retiring and the new leadership, new CEO did not want me. I will never forget those hours in the hotel room. I have never ever cried that much in my life. It was as if all the tears I had were drained out of me. I could not see God or feel God's presence with me. I felt very alone and began questioning what God was doing to me.

Upon my return home the "exit strategy" was being developed and the communication was being written to announce my departure. I could not share any details; I was told to just leave quietly. So I did. Afterward, my family and I dealt with anger, frustration, planning demise, and the list goes on. My last days were very difficult partly because I had no idea what I was going to do. I had loved my position and I had loved the organization that no longer had a place for me.

Let me go back to life "before" for a moment. Life was good. I had a job that I thought would be mine forever; I loved my job and my career. I had worked hard to advance in my profession and felt successful in my career. My husband, Mike and I enjoyed involvement in our community; we enjoyed being a part of the community. Our daughter, Makila kept us busy with the usual activities of a second grader with little league, playmates, and trying to raise her well in today's challenging world. I was the model church lady. I was there about every time the doors were open, Bible study (teaching and participating), committee meetings, Sunday services, Sunday school, VBS, and a variety of other acts of service. The church secretary knew me by name. Makila had been raised in the church attending preschool, Sunday school, and VBS. I made sure she knew the church. "It takes a village" did not miss our family. She was very much at home at our church. One Easter she began to tell me the Easter story on our way to preschool and didn't miss a line, how happy I was! Mike was part of the church; Makila and I made sure he became a part of the church, (O.K., that's another testimony).

I had a great relationship with the church and thought my relationship with God was where I wanted it to be. I wanted it to be. Let me say that one more time,,, where I wanted it to be. Did I mention that I knew church; as any good Methodist, I could recite the Apostle's Creed without looking in the hymnal and the Doxology too. Did I mention how much I loved my career, my job and the involvement in our community? And that **my** relationship with God was where I thought it needed to be?

In early 2008 I was privileged to go on my first mission trip. Now, I don't start small so this first trip was to Uganda, Africa. It was an amazing trip and one that began a lifelong passion in me. When I look back, I know that God was all over this trip for me. I was blessed to go with some amazing people that mentored me and became lifelong friends. It was during the trip I texted Mike to say that I had seen the face of God. This was so true! His face was in the women that I met who had stepped out of their lives to be mothers to the orphans in the villages. One mother shared with me that she went to her pastor after a service that shared the Uganda orphan's stories and she knew that God had asked her to give her life to these orphans. The simplicity of these mothers' faith, the joy brought by a pair of reading glasses to read a Bible and the love in their faces as we talked about the joy of our Savior affected me deeply.

Not long after this trip my husband and I participated in a faith weekend retreat called Emmaus. The Walk to Emmaus is an experience of Christian spiritual renewal and formation. It is an opportunity to meet Jesus Christ in a new way, as God's grace and love is revealed through fellow believers. It is a wonderful faith growing experience. I had wanted Mike to go on this retreat for a couple of years so when he finally said yes, "we went!" Now I didn't quite get what I expected,,, I got so much more. Mike grew in his relationship with God with this experience and our relationship grew and changed more than we could have ever dreamed. Mike began to teach and speak for Bible studies and church events. Our relationship with the church grew even more as a family.

Both the Uganda mission trip and the Walk to Emmaus experiences were wonderful and added to my career and family, well that was where I wanted to be in life...

And to add a little icing to the cake, we bought a new house, we were the first occupants of this house and it was our dream home. Life was good.

Now, I don't want to say our life was "charmed", both Mike and I were in demanding jobs that at times required a great deal of our time, but we were good. We were blessed with family support and we were growing in our faith.

Switching back to life, "after", life changed for us as we knew it. I went through a period of depression (more than I had admitted during this time); I put on my happy face and carried out the masquerade to perpetuate what everyone outside of my family believed was the story. This life altering process occurred in the fall, right before the holidays, since we had the time, we put on our smiles and so hosted Mike's side of the family for Thanksgiving and my side for Christmas. Makila was happy to have mom home after school every day with snacks and conversation. After the holiday gatherings, the Sunday school party, and Makila's New Year's Eve slumber party, the house organizing projects became smaller and smaller, then it hit me "What Am I Going To DO?!!!!"

I am not a stay at home person never have been, never will be. The job possibilities that I thought would be there weren't; and those that were involved a move. We wanted to stay where we were, Mike's job was good and Makila was happy in school plus we were in a house we loved besides we didn't know how it would sell!!!

There were wounds, deep wounds that I didn't know how to heal. I would say that there hadn't just been knifes in my back, there had been *butcher knives*, and it would take some time, maybe a lot of time, for the healing to begin.

I had attended a Beth Moore Living Proof conference with my mother and one of my Christian sisters. In her message, Beth talked about trusting God and how He looks at us with questions, "You don't trust **Me** with this???" I put that question all over my house, little strips of paper with this phrase and the "**Me**" in red, I was talking to God, I wanted to trust Him. I looked at them, I read them daily but was I really applying them to my life? Apparently not!

I thought I was trusting God but I was really waiting for a job to fall into my lap or just hit me in the face.

Then I made a conscious decision; to work closer with God through prayer and develop a plan. The work became more diligent with a recruiter and trying to find the right job for me. God's got to be part of the plan or there isn't one. Mike's job was very stressful and he was very good at what he did, that gave us comfort that he could find work whenever and wherever we should move. We revised the search for my job by trying to stay close to our families, but not more than one state away from Oklahoma.

Then one morning I awoke very early with severe right abdominal pain. I thought maybe I had eaten something that didn't set right with me. With my direction from bed, Mike was able to get our daughter off to school. But as he was getting ready for work the pain kept increasing and I started thinking,,,this isn't a simple tummy ache. Now being a nurse I began my assessment and informed Mike that I felt I needed to go to the Emergency Room because I was having appendicitis. I was diagnosed with severe appendicitis and needed an immediate appendectomy to prevent a ruptured appendix.

O.K., what now? I couldn't believe this, yet it was all very real. It was hard to understand how this was happening, right now when I felt I was going on the right path and had focus. He had to put me in bed. God gave me more time, time to be still, be still and listen. He was preparing a place for us, in the midst of this physical set-back.

During my recovery from surgery Mike and I had conversations about the possibility of needing to move farther away from Oklahoma than our one-state-away plan allowed as there did not seem to be much opportunity close to home and family. Did I mention how important family is to our lives? We were prayerful and soon made the decision to expand the geographic region for our job search with the expectation that there had to be good jobs for both of us and a good school for our daughter.

Looking at career postings and talking with recruiters there seemed to be a flow of opportunities in a certain state on the east coast. We lived in the middle of the country. How were we going to function so far away from family? Did I mention how important family is to our lives? The pull kept coming, O.K. God, *is this where we are supposed to go? Why? Why?*

Now, understand I had filled out many applications, sent many resumes, and had multiple phone interviews with little advancement in process. Then another opportunity in this east coast state came; the process went from a Skype interview to travel for site interview in less than two weeks. Other applications had been unanswered for months or elicited no response at all. During the site interview everything felt right, it clicked, and it felt good. Mike jokes that I had texted him with, "they have a Target," so he thought then the move was a done deal. When I began the flight home I had my usual prayer for safe air travel with little turbulence and added plea to understand why this opportunity felt so right.

The second site interview involved Mike traveling with me. Our daughter remained at home with grandma in charge and it was a good time for Mike to get away for some much needed rest. It was important for him to see what was drawing me to this place so far away from the Heartland. During our travel we continued discussing our commitment that there had to be good jobs for both of us and a good school for our daughter.

We went through the whirlwind visit with Mike meeting the team I would be working with, going to a variety of places in this community to get "a feel" of the people and looking for job opportunities for him. It was a good visit. When we were in the car driving to the airport to return home when I turned to Mike and asked the all-important question "What did you think?" and he responded "We're moving to North Carolina." I was shocked and surprised; he hadn't found a job and didn't see much opportunity in his career area. What about our commitment to find something for *both* of us? What about this being the place for *all* of us?

This conversation led both of us to acknowledge that we felt strongly that God was leading us away from Oklahoma and placing us in North Carolina. Our prayers continued asking God to show us this path if this is to be part of our journey.

Letting God lead and trusting God to take care of us, the plan unfolded and we could see the direction He was leading us in.

How was the plan revealed to us? Well, the house sold the first week on the market, the school that we visited made a good impression, and the job offer was generous. Yet. There was nothing for Mike. Still, we trusted and we moved forward, beginning our journey to North Carolina.

Things were happening so quickly. I would be leaving the day after Makila's 8th birthday to start the new job. Mike would be closing things down in Oklahoma and Makila would travel east with grandparents. I don't want to paint a picture that everything was sunshine and smiles. Our daughter wasn't buying this adventure that mom and dad was taking her on. According to her, I was devastating her life, taking her away from everyone and everything that she knew and loved. In my best motherly tone I informed her that she was 7, and she had a great deal of life ahead for her. For some reason she didn't buy it.

In her defense, we were leaving my brother and his family that lived in the same community and this included her cousin that she had spent those 7 years growing up with would now be half away across the country. Did I mention how important family is to us? Additionally our church family was very difficult to leave, we loved being with them so much, and we grieved the loss. We learned that a strong church family never is ever very far away and they continue to share their prayers and love for us.

In the days before I left I had lunch with my best friend, Melissa, and we shared the excitement of the journey and tears of the distance, not really goodbye just how far away we would be from each other. Thank goodness for our technology age with texting, Facebook, email and phone calls. During our lunch she asked me a question that has been with me and stays with me through every situation, "What did you learn during this time?"

As I began the drive eastward, I saw God all the way during my journey. There was not just one incident, I gave myself time to stop and see family and friends on my way out of state; and I stayed in contact with Melissa texting and calls, while stopped. As I crossed the states lines on my drive there were crosses strategically placed along the highway whenever I needed them to give me encouragement. Thank you, God!

> *"My flesh and my heart may fail, but God is the strength of my heart and my portion forever. Those who are far from you will perish; you destroy all who are unfaithful to you. But as for me, it is good to be near God; I have made the Sovereign Lord my refuge, I will tell of all your deeds."* Psalm 73:26-28 (NIV)

I share all of this with you to start you on the personal journey of knowing what it means to trust God with everything in your life, every circumstance, every area and every single day—being close to God.

He is amazing and has amazing things planned for you and for me.

Talk Time

1. *Trust in the Lord, and do good; Dwell in the land, and feed on His faithfulness.* Psalm 37:3 (NKJV)

   Read trust in God's word. What does the word trust bring to your mind when you read it in this verse?

2. What relationship(s) in your life do you consider "trustworthy" and why?

3. *But look, you are trusting in deceptive words that are worthless. Will you steal and murder, commit adultery and perjury, burn incense to Baal and follow other gods you have not known, and then come and stand before me in this house, which bears my Name, and say, "We are safe"--safe to do all these detestable things?" Jeremiah 7:8-10 (NIV)*

This is God's message to the people of Judah, their indifference and rebellion against God. You can sense His frustration with them and their ways. They have not trusted Him.

Have you ever had a situation where trust was broken? How did that make you feel? Did it change the relationship?

Have you ever broken someone's trust?

chapter
two

The Verse, The Whole Verse

During our goodbyes, when Melissa asked me that question, "What did you learn during this time?" I just stopped and thought, "I really hadn't thought about *learning* anything." Then it came to me as if I had it all along, and I answered her, "to trust in God." She just smiled at me. In the coming days I reflected on my answer and the verse that continues to be a vital part of my faith. In Proverbs 3:5 we are told to *"Trust in the Lord with all our heart, and do not lean on our own understanding."* (ESV)

At one time I felt that verse only had one thing to say, to trust in the Lord with all my heart. That was it, nothing more than saying I trust in Him with all my heart. Yet, we must complete the verse to put the whole wisdom into perspective; trust in Him and not our own understanding. That can lead to some challenges for those of us that like to be in control, do I hear an "Amen"?

Let's divide this verse into the two parts to study how we are to trust God. Let's start with the word *trust*. How do we consider trust in our everyday world? Do we consider with question and caution?

In sharing this story I recall how trust had been greatly broken in my world. People that I had worked with for a number of years as colleagues and co-workers now represented broken relationships that were possibly never to be repaired. It was the knife in my back that felt like a butcher knife with a slash so big it would never heal enough to leave a scar; forever open and hurting with salt being poured in it. Things were spoken against me, I had no support, I was undermined, subordinates had their own agenda, and it was difficult to lead and effect change in my work environment. I had specifically asked a leader for support and mentorship only to have them turn on me. Trust was not an easy word to keep in my life.

My story was in the work environment, where is yours? Have you had a relationship that you thought was the bomb only to find out that your words have been twisted or misquoted? What about the boyfriend, husband, and friend with whom you thought the relationship was forever, you gave them your heart and they broke it. Could your mistrust be due to a parent that left you, a sibling that lied, a child that let you down or best friend that is no longer? Or is it a repair shop that hasn't fixed your car right; time after time they said to trust them with your car. Trust has many faces in our world that go from the routine day to the extreme in relationships; some small enough that we will never use that repair shop again some as monumental as a damaged broken relationship that leaves scars and destroys trust in another.

There is more than one situation in all of our lives where trust has been broken How are we expected to trust God when we can't trust those we are around every day? How? He is more than our everyday world.

> *I have told you these things, so that in me you may have peace. In this world you will have trouble. But take heart! I have overcome the world.* John 16:33 (NIV)

To learn and grow in our knowledge of the words spoken to us I want to take us to the detail of those words. Early in my Bible study days when anyone would say that they had the Hebrew or Greek definition for a word it would just go right over my head. Why would I want to know other words for what I read in the Bible? I don't understand the Hebrew or Greek pronunciation and I don't know how I would use it in daily conversation. I have since been enlightened to this knowledge, thank you God! The ancient language gives us the deeper meaning of the word by putting the word into perspective of the time in which it was written for us to apply today. John 1:5 tells us that

> *"the light shines in the darkness, and the darkness has not overcome it."* (NIV)

We become brighter as faithful people learning more and getting deeper with God.

Defining trust by the world's definition we go to the dictionary which says that trust is: 1 *a*: assured reliance on the character, ability, strength, or truth of someone or something and *b*: one in which confidence is placed. (1) These definitions sound as if trust is earned not by faith but by showing character, ability or strength then you place your confidence.

In the Proverbs verse we are discussing the word *trust* is a Hebrew word, *batah*. This is figuratively to trust, be confident or sure---be secure, be confident. (2) This seems to be more definitive, **be** confident and **be** secure. It is not asking us to place our confidence in something, it is telling us to **be** confident.

Man says, "Show me, and I'll trust you." God says, "Trust Me, and I'll show you."

Looking at Proverbs we know that this is a book of wisdom. It is a book of wise sayings about everyday life. Proverbs is considered an "Owner's Manual for Life", rules for everyday living. Most of the proverbs are credited to Solomon who had a passion for knowledge and wisdom. Solomon was world known as many came from all over to hear him. He was a scientist, a political ruler, a businessman with vast enterprises, a poet, moralist, and preacher. (3) The first chapters are credited to Solomon. Proverbs chapter 3 may have been written in Solomon's time but it has application for our everyday life all through it.

Proverbs 3: 5a says *"Trust in the Lord with all our heart."* When we put the words from our Hebrew definition in place we get *"**Be** confident in the Lord with all our heart"* or *"**Be** secure in the Lord with all our heart."* That seems pretty direct with little room for question as to what we are to **be**, is confident and secure in the Lord.

I would like to challenge you as you read the Bible to replace the word "trust" with "be confident" or "be secure," feel the connection you will have with God when you do this.

To fully grasp the trust we are to have in God is to begin letting God *lead* your life, not just be a part of your life. He is leading you, all of your life. 1Peter 5:10 is the best perspective,

> *And the God of all grace, who called you to his eternal glory in Christ, after you have suffered a little while, will himself restore you and make you strong, firm and steadfast.* (NIV)

God loves, God helps, God fights, and God wins. When we give God our suffering, our disappointments, our sorrow, our misery, our fears and our troubles He will wrap us in His love and grace. He will pour His love into us for healing and strength.

> *If the Lord had not been my help, my soul would soon have lived in the land of silence. When I thought, My foot slips, your steadfast love, O Lord, held me up. When the cares of my heart many, your consolations cheer my soul.*
> Psalm 94: 17-19 (ESV)

We are to make the decision that God is leading our life not just a part of our life on Sunday or occasional Bible study or special event but every day, all day and all night, always. He is our help.

> Trust (**Be** confident) in him at all times,
> O people; pour out your hearts to him,
> for God is our refuge. Psalms 62:8 (NIV)
> (emphasis added)

Let God lead your life, He is the shelter in the storm.

When He leads your life you do not lean on your own understanding. Those of us that have control issues can see this as life changing or it can be life saving.

Proverbs 3:5b states, "*do not lean on your own understanding.*" For those words are specific and to the point, but let's break them down.

"*Do not,*" most of us have said that to our children or spouse in a very firm tone that leaves little room for question.

"*Lean,*" may seem relaxing but in this text it is that we do not rely, count on, or look to our self. The word understanding has possibilities that come to our mind of knowledge limited to a specific skill, comprehending a problem presented to us or maybe to simply know what is meant by a statement.

"*Understanding,*" in the Hebrew language is *binah* which is from the root *bin. Bin* is to separate mentally or distinguish, understand. The list of words to describe understanding begins and covers quite a list—attend, diligently, direct, discern, eloquent, inform, instruct, have intelligence, know, look well to, mark, perceive, be prudent, regard skillful, teach, think,,,,,, The Hebrew definition of *binah*, and remember *bin* is the root, is few words—knowledge, meaning, perfectly, understanding, wisdom. Do you see perfect wisdom when you see God? His wisdom is perfect, ours is not. Our wisdom is limited and we know that because if our wisdom was perfect we wouldn't be in some of our situations, messes, and disappointing circumstances.

We are to be confident and sure in the Lord with all our heart for His perfect wisdom. Sounds doable to me, how about you? Maybe? Remember, let God lead your life.

> *In all your ways acknowledge him,*
> *and he will make straight your paths.*
> Proverbs 3:6 (ESV)

Proverbs 3:5 and 3:6 together give us clear direction. Trust in Him, be confident, and be sure with everything and acknowledge Him. He has the directions and knows every road.

There are many people of the Bible that give examples of trust through life and trials. Consider Jeremiah, he is someone that kings trusted and he advised and then he was shackled and imprisoned. Like Jeremiah we have been on the inner circles, part of the decision making process only to find that there were those that wanted you out? Jeremiah trusted God in prison, in the cistern, filth, shackles and chains. He trusted God and knew God was taking care of him. Our situations can't be worse than Jeremiah's. In the chapters of Jeremiah there is the fall of the kingdoms of Judah and Jerusalem. Jeremiah was the prophet, the spokesperson for God to the people preparing them for this fall; not good news. His advice for the people after the fall is to be obedient and peaceful; the word that came from the Lord was,

> "*For surely I know the plans I have for you, says the Lord, plans for your welfare and not for harm, to give you a future with hope. Then when you call upon me and come and pray to me, I will hear you. When you search for me, you will find me; if you seek me with your whole heart.*" Jeremiah 29:11-13 (NOAB)

Through these verses we gain great understanding of the Lord but let's examine our role. Did you see "seek with your whole heart"? He wants us whole, every part of us; we must choose to let God lead our life. When we seek Him with our whole heart, we will find Him.

Jeremiah had what some would see has a hopeless mission. He didn't have good news to share and he suffered a great deal through the delivery of the message. He expressed his anger and frustration with the Lord for the afflictions and suffering but he didn't leave. He calls his afflictions "wormwood and gall", YUK!! When we read his poem in Lamentations 3:22-24 we see that Jeremiah didn't give up hope or faith, he knew God's loyalties.

> *The steadfast love of the Lord never ceases his mercies never come to an end; they are new every morning; great is your faithfulness. "The Lord is my portion, says my soul, "therefore I will hope in him."* Lamentations 3:22-24(NOAB)

God's steadfast love **never** ceases, never stops, His mercies **never** come to an end, and they are forever. That is something to **be** confident of our lives. The word *never* is an adverb to mean at no time in the past or future; on no occasion; not ever; absolutely not, that's God. God stood with Jeremiah during his many disappointments and persecutions; we can expect the same from God to do for us, to stand with us always. On no occasion will His mercies come to an end for us.

My wounds took time to heal with some of the smaller wounds healing first. God was working in me and I was working to let God lead my life with my whole heart. I knew that He was standing with me; I just needed to begin to trust, so the scars began to form. The scars are my testimony and that is how He is surely making me His vessel.

> *Commit your way to the Lord; trust in him...* Psalm 37:5a (NIV)

There is a wonderful book by Hannah Whitall Smith called "The God of All Comfort". In this book she tells us:

> *We are "God's workmanship," and God is good, therefore His workmanship must be good also; and we may securely **trust** that before He is done with us, He will make us out of something that will be to His glory, no matter how unlike this we may as yet feel ourselves to be. (4)*

Talk Time

1. Where has mistrust occurred in your life? Minor or Major? How is that relationship now?

2. To be confident, be secure: *batah.* Considering the definition for trust, how do you compare your understanding of trust with trusting God?

3. *"Before I formed you in the womb I knew you, before you were born I set you apart; I appointed you as a prophet to the nations." "Ah, Sovereign Lord," I said, "I do not know how to speak; I am only a child." But the Lord said to me, "Do not say, 'I am only a child.' You must go to everyone I send you to and say whatever I command you. Do not be afraid of them, for I am with you and will rescue you," declares the Lord.* Jeremiah 1:5-8 (NIV)

Considering Jeremiah's life, would you be able to trust that God is right beside you in prison, in the cistern, in your worst situation?

three

Here We Go...

As I left my story in the first chapter we were starting our journey to North Carolina. The house in Oklahoma had sold but we had not found a place to live in North Carolina nor had we not yet rented another property we owned in Oklahoma. Mike stressed and worried about the rental until the day that he left for his journey to North Carolina. We had not had good luck with reliable renters and he did not want to be 1300 miles away with bad renters, meantime I was looking for a house in North Carolina.

It was 2008, and the economy had started to shift related to mortgage companies and buying homes. Once we found a house and the purchase process began, it was different than other times we had been through with the mortgage process. I filled out paperwork and had to provide documentation that was still packed away in Oklahoma. There seemed to be more "hoops to jump through" than previously in the process. Finally the house bought, movers were scheduled and Mike oversaw the movers, after they loaded our belongings, he left for his journey to North Carolina.

On the day that he left Oklahoma, he rented the house. A couple that was going through a difficult time with the loss of a child needed a placed to live. We knew them as Mike and the husband were good friends. They shook hands on the deal and Mike headed east stopping along the way to visit with family and friends.

Mike and furniture arrived and we began to settle into our new life. Makila arrived with grandparents a few weeks later and by the middle of August we were all in North Carolina. Mike started looking for employment opportunities after we got Makila settled in school. The hard part was taking granddad and grandma to the airport and saying good bye. Did I mention how important family is to us? As a family we had not lived so far from family members and her grandparents did not want to be so far from their only granddaughter.

Mike and I had committed to searching for our next home church. We wanted to find a church that would be good for Makila and be a good fit for the whole family. The search started but it didn't seem that we visited many churches. We would visit one church, and then another but then go back to the first and then visit another. This went on for a month or so and then it was realized that we keep returning to the first church. A new pastor had started about the time that we had started our search and we kept going back again and again.

A story we like to share is when we visited a church we assumed it would be like our home church in Oklahoma. Each church was different in their summer schedule and dress, and Mike dressed in "normal" summer style; no suit or tie; the "new" church was in full dress. All men were in suits, so yes we got some looks. Then with another church we visited Mike went in a suit only to find that the dress was summer style; floral or beach prints and no suits or even ties. Needless to say he was getting confused and a little frustrated.

The frustration, we missed our home church. Yet we kept going back to the first church. We couldn't identify exactly why or what was drawing us to this church. It was deep in Methodist tradition; there was not a contemporary service or much talk about starting a contemporary service. It had a strong children's program, even though none of children were in Makila's school she seemed to be happy. There are a number of elementary schools in the county so not everyone was from the same school. On one of our visits a peppy friendly lady asked us what school Makila attended.

When church was over she came and took Makila to meet one of the teachers from her new school. A co-worker of mine had also shared with another teacher that Makila would be coming to her school. We felt good about the connection with teachers and Makila's adjustment to a new school.

As for the service, we were not unfamiliar with a traditional service but we had been involved with the start of the contemporary service at our home church. Mike played the guitar back home and loves contemporary music. Mike and I began to sense a strong connection with the new pastor and his wife. The messages were powerful and full of scripture. We made the decision to make this our North Carolina home church and joined the congregation. Once it was found out that Mike was musical he was invited to join the choir. We felt a connection but knew that the tradition was deep at this church and it might take some time and effort to become part of the church. In our reflection back at the early days in North Carolina we thank God for this wonderful church family. They were not "just" a church family they become our North Carolina family. God richly blessed us.

Life began to settle down and we were making North Carolina a home, though granddad made sure Makila did not run out of Oklahoma t-shirts. We missed Oklahoma but knew that God had led us to a new chapter in our life journey, specifically our faith walk.

The first year had its share of ups and downs with what seemed to be more downs than ups. I loved my new position and felt a great connection with the people at the organization. Makila adjusted fairly well in her new school. She missed family, a lot. Mike was struggling with finding employment and began showing signs of depression. He left an industry in which he had worked very hard to attain a high level of exposure and community involvement. It was a big change for him because the industry in North Carolina was different and he did not have the reputation that he had in his previous position. He began to have health problems related to his chronic battle with diabetes and weight. Mike had been diagnosed at one time as being "morbidly obese" and this contributed to the problems he had with diabetes. I know God was taking care of Mike through this time off but Mike didn't see it at the time. He enjoyed singing in the choir but missed playing the guitar.

One Sunday there is a special presentation of the African Children's Choir with a video showing the area of Africa that I had traveled to on my first mission trip. The presentation was for a ministry that was different from what I had shared in, but my heart jumped, flipped and quivered hearing the story and the mission of this ministry. Our church was being asked to participate in the ministry. Mike looked at me, saw my face and said, "You're going back to Africa?" My response, "Looks like it." I had been struggling with my involvement in our church having been previously very involved with missions, women's ministry, children's ministry, education and committees. I did not have much involvement in our new church at all. It seemed odd to not be deeply involved but I knew God had a plan for me. I just had to listen for His direction and not try to do it on my own. In reflecting on this time I recognized that there was a difference in what God had in store for me this time. I was learning to let go, He was pruning. I didn't have to do everything I thought I should do at church. I needed to focus, not just become another "church lady," again. The Master Gardner wants us to be productive in our service. He will prune the unproductive energy in our life so that we can become fruitful servants in His kingdom.

> *I am the true vine, and my Father is the vinedresser. Every branch in me that does not bear fruit he takes away, and every branch that does bear fruit he prunes, that it may bear more fruit.* John 15:1-2 (ESV)

In summarizing our first year in this place called North Carolina that we never thought we would live yet we trusted that we were where God wanted us to be. We were learning just how God is faithful in all our circumstances.

How do we trust that God is faithful? He has been faithful in the past. In the Old Testament we have many stories of His faithfulness. David praises God for his faithfulness in many of the Psalm and in the New Testament Paul recounts God's faithfulness to Moses in his letter to the church at Corinth.

In the book of Judges there is the story of Gideon, who was called by God to defeat a group of people that were not very nice to the Israelites, the Midianites. The part of the story that we are the most familiar with is when Gideon was called by God and he responded to God by questioning His selection:

> *But sir, how can I deliver Israel? My clan is the weakest in Manasseh, and I am the least for my family.* Judges 6:15 (ESV)

God responds that He will be with him; But Gideon is not too sure so he tests God with the fleece test as found in Judges 6:17-40.

The conversation that is not always highlighted is when the angel of the Lord first appears to Gideon and says to him,

> *"The Lord is with you, you mighty warrior." To which Gideon answers, "But sir, if the Lord is with us, why then has all this happened to us? And where are all his wonderful deeds that our ancestors recounted to us?"* Judges 6:11-13 (ESV).

Gideon is asking why all of "this" is happening, questioning where God has been and whether God has even heard their cries. Don't we ask the same questions during our time of challenges and tribulation? When this started in 2008, that was my question, why did this happen to me, and why did it take so long to find that right job? Where was God in all of this?

God answered the Israelites call by calling Gideon to deliver them from the Midianites. Gideon had questions, not just about his ability but where had God been when things weren't going so well for the Israelites over the past 7 years. God qualified Gideon to defeat the Midianites and He will qualify us in our life to face the tribulation and challenges that come our way. God is faithful.

The Israelites had been in bondage for 7 years at the hand of the Midianites. The Midianites oppressed the Israelites by destroying their crops and taking their livestock. The land was invaded by the Midianites and ravaged beyond productive use for crops or livestock.

They sought refuge in caves and built pits to hide their grain in protection from the raids by the Midianites. "*...the people of Israel cried out for help to the Lord.*" Judges 6:6b (ESV)

Can you imagine 7 years? Panic sets in at 7 days for most of us with some of us it's within minutes when we are presented with a challenge, change or set back that we panic.

In Judges we see that God delivered the Israelites seven times. Before Gideon the Lord has delivered the Israelites 3 times. Judges begins after the great leader Joshua has died and there is no leader to take his place. During this period the Israelites are going through six major judge cycles. Three occurred before Gideon and they include Othniel, Ehud and Deborah. In each period of time the Israelites are oppressed and cry out to the Lord for deliverance. Each time they cry out and the Lord provides a deliverer and the spirit of the Lord is upon the deliverer to subdue the oppressor. God is faithful.

In the Old Testament we have the prophet Habakkuk. He calls out to God for help. Asking how long God is going to keep letting this world be so bad. The society that Habakkuk is talking about is violent, corrupt and wicked. They have a dialogue back and forth with Habakkuk crying out and God answering him. He sees no end to the bad things that are happening in his world and questions God. Are you listening? Don't you hear the cries? Why must we go on with this?

This goes back and forth when in God's response it is said ",,,*but the righteous will live by his faith,*" Habakkuk 2:4 (NIV).

Habakkuk's prayer in the third chapter of Habakkuk, it is a beautiful reply for us in our situations and the confidence of our faith. Habakkuk recounts what God has done in the past and looks with faith to what God will do for the outcome. In the closing of the prayer Habakkuk rejoices in the Lord and knows that his strength comes from the Sovereign Lord.

> *Though the fig tree does not bud and*
> *there are no grapes on the vines,*
> *though the olive crop fails and the fields*
> *produce no food,*
> *though there are no sheep in the pen and*
> *no cattle in the stalls,*
> *yet I will rejoice in the Lord,*
> *I will be joyful in God my Savior.*
> *The Sovereign Lord is my strength;*
> *he makes my feet like the feet of a deer,*
> *he enables me to go on the heights.*
> Habakkuk 3:17-19 (NIV)

Talk Time

1. What are your questions of God during those times of tribulation, challenges or struggles? What is your "panic" timeline?

2. *"And all that generations also were gathered to their fathers. And there arose another generation after them who did not know the Lord or the work that he had done for Israel. And the people of Israel did what was evil in the sight of the Lord and served the Baals. And they abandoned the Lord, the God of their fathers, who had brought them out of the land of Egypt. They went after other gods, from among the gods of the peoples who were around them, and bowed down to them. And they provoked the Lord to anger. They abandoned the Lord and served the Baals and the Ashtaroth."* Judges 2:10-13 *(ESV)*

    What were the Israelites doing to God? Why were they doing this to God?

3. *"Therefore know that the Lord your God, He is God, the faithful God who keeps covenant and mercy for a thousand generations with those who love Him and keep His commandments:"* Deuteronomy 7:9 (NKJV) When it is said in this verse that "He is the faithful God", what emotions come to your thoughts?

4. Write out a prayer for yourself acknowledging God's faithfulness in your life using Habakkuk's prayer.

chapter
four

Our World in The Bible

I have talked about Gideon and Habakkuk. Let's take another person from the Old Testament, Joseph. You may remember him from your childhood Sunday school and VBS teachings about his coat of many colors. There is a part about Joseph that can be related to situations in our lives today.

The first connection observed about Joseph was his life prior to his brothers selling him to the Egyptians. He had it pretty good and he was confident in his life with his father Israel (Jacob).

> *Now Israel loved Joseph more than*
> *any of his other sons, because he had*
> *been born to him in his old age, and he*
> *made a richly ornamented robe for him.*
> Genesis 37:3 (NIV)

There's that coat of many colors. Joseph was confident as a 17 year old and he was a little cocky in his relationship with his father.

Joseph got himself in trouble with his brothers when he tattled on them for how they were "tending" the sheep and he shared dreams he had about them bowing down **to** him. Even his father rebuked him but didn't do so in front of the brothers (Gen 37:10-11). Israel's fondness for Joseph plus Joseph's own attitude may have led to the envy and hatred by his brothers. The brothers had had enough and made the decision to develop a plot to kill him. Fortunately for Joseph one of his brothers, Reuben, didn't want to kill him so he suggested that they throw him into the cistern in the desert and leave him.

Just as I mentioned previously I was pretty satisfied with my life, great husband, beautiful daughter, loving family, loving church family, great job, etc......Then things changed for me about like they did for Joseph. I wasn't quite thrown in the cistern but it sure felt like it during those trying days.

Cistern is from the Hebrew word *bor*, which means a receptacle for water delivered to it either from an external spring or a rain-fall. Cisterns are mentioned frequently in scripture related to the dryness of the summer months and scarcity of springs in Judea. The cisterns have a round opening at the top, sometimes built up with stonework. Empty cisterns were used for prisons and places of confinement, as with Joseph. It is an assumption that the empty cistern was not a pleasant place. Depending on how long it had been empty it would not have been very well cared for and would have been a home for bugs and other unpleasant things plus the stonework would be jagged and could hurt a person on the way down. Let's say Joseph was not in a good place, physically or emotionally. Not only was he in this pit but he was there because his brothers put him there.

The brothers decided to sell Joseph to some Midianite merchants who happened by on their way to Egypt. Joseph was sold to the merchants for 20 shekels of silver which is only about $158 in the 2014 market, talk about an insult!

> *So when the Midianite merchants came by, his brothers pulled Joseph up out of the cistern and sold him for twenty shekels of silver to the Ishmaelites, who took him to Egypt.* Genesis 37:28 (NIV)

Joseph was now on his way to Egypt. This was not a very pleasant trip being tied to a rope behind a camel, plus he didn't have plans or a need to go to Egypt. Life was getting ready to change in a big way for Joseph.

In the words of Max Lucado, *"You'll get through this. It won't be painless. It won't be quick. But God will use this mess for good. In the meantime don't be foolish or naïve. But don't despair either. With God's help you will get through this."* (5)

In looking at Joseph's story we are going to understand this statement and see that our pit is not much different than Joseph.

> *"Joseph would be the first to tell you that life in the pit stinks. Yet for all its rottenness doesn't the pit do this much? It forces you to look upward. Someone from up there must come down here and give you a hand. God did for Joseph. At the right time, in the right way, he will do the same for you."* (5)

Joseph was on his way to Egypt. Once in Egypt the Midianites sold Joseph to Potiphar the captain of Pharaoh's guard. Life in Egypt was good for Joseph, not great, but good because the Lord was with him. In chapter 39 of Genesis we are told clearly that "the Lord

was with Joseph", it is stated four times in the verses
of chapter 39. The last verse says, *",,, because the Lord
was with Joseph and gave him success in whatever he
did." Genesis 39:23 (NIV)*

Joseph faced Potiphar's wife, prison, and betrayal
by the cupbearer and the baker, all in all not a very
comfortable life in Egypt for Joseph—plus he hadn't
planned on going to Egypt in the first place.

The first year in North Carolina was like Joseph in
Egypt; good but, not great. It was good because the
Lord was with us. Now, we didn't have Potiphar's wife
or the cupbearer and baker but we had challenges
during that first year that had me questioning our
move. Mike was not able to find full time work and
his health was not good. Makila struggled with her
new school and would many times ask when we were
going back to Oklahoma. We missed our families and
our church home. Mike and I knew that God was with
us during this time and during the times of doubt
and question we could see that God was with us and
leading us. It was during this time-period that we fully
began to trust God and knew that He had a plan for
us. We often responded to the question, "Why did you
come to North Carolina? We followed God."

At one such event there was a lady, who became
one of our dearest friends, who asked me during our

conversation, "How long are you going to stay in North Carolina?" I was taken by surprise and responded blankly, "I don't know". The conversation stayed in my mind and I now know that my better response should have been, "I don't know, we didn't plan on coming to NC, God brought us here, it's His decision when we leave."

It is always a great value when we can look back and reflect on events in our life. The first year and half were hard and we faced challenges of being out of our comfort zone. A zone not only without family, but our friends and connections that was solid in Oklahoma. It was different in North Carolina. What did God teach us? He taught us the value of new friends who became our NC family and our growth as a family. We saw what happens when we trust God; our trust grows as our faith grows, and we experience God's faithfulness. The three of us are tight. We strengthened ourselves as a family and grew in our faith as a family during our first year on the east coast.

Just like Joseph settled into life in Egypt, we settled into life in North Carolina. After that first year Makila began to settle in at school and activities out of school. Mike made a decision about his health after he received a serious scare in a conversation with his new physician. The diabetes was taking its toll on Mike's body and he needed to lose weight and lose it not only permanently but also quickly to make an impact on his health. He was told that he didn't have to worry about his daughter's wedding because he would not see her high school graduation in his current condition.

We also came to enjoy the beautiful coastal shores of North Carolina and often made trips to the beach for our family retreats. Our church home became a place of activity for all of us and grew to be our NC family.

Joseph settled in Egypt after he was brought out of prison to interpret Pharaoh's dreams. Pharaoh saw the spirit of God in Joseph and asked all his officials,

> *"Can we find anyone like this man,*
> *one in whom is the spirit of God?"*
> Genesis 41:38 (NIV)

Pharaoh placed Joseph in his service. Joseph married and had two sons both named for the glory of what God had done in Joseph's life.

Framed in Faith

> One was named Manasseh and Joseph said, "It is because God has made me forget all my trouble and all my father's household." And the second was named Ephraim and said, "It is because God has made me fruitful in the land of my suffering." Genesis 41:51-52 (NIV)

Joseph knew throughout his time in Egypt that God was with him. His faith was strong and growing stronger. Talking to his brother he said:

> "So then, it was not you who sent me here, but God." Genesis 45:8 (NIV).

We felt that God had led us to North Carolina and placed us there for His purpose. There were times that we questioned what the purpose was and we knew that the answer would come in God's time, we may see it, and we may not.

The story of Joseph shows us, teaches us that God is faithful and we are to trust in Him. I knew that prior to our move to NC God was teaching me to trust in Him; that was only the beginning of the lesson. Learning more about Joseph helps to see that what is intended for our hardship; that God can turn our pit into something glorious and wonderful, a Masterpiece

49

for good. God is working in our time just as He worked in Egypt during Joseph's time.

> "We can't always see what God is doing, but can't we assume he is up to something good? Joseph did. He assumed God was in the crisis." (5)

God tells us this in the Old Testament and the New Testament:

> *God tells us, "For the heavens are higher than the earth, so are my ways higher than your ways and my thoughts than your thoughts."* Isaiah 55:9 (ESV)

> Paul tells us, *"Now to him who is able to do far more abundantly than all that we ask or think, according to the power at work within us".* Ephesians 3:20 (ESV)

He has got us in his arms and His plans are amazing for us.

Let's return to Jeremiah's story in the Old Testament. He was someone who did not have an easy path as a prophet. The news that he delivered was not good because it was the last plea from God for Jerusalem. They were a community who worshiped idols and were not obedient to God. Jeremiah was not looked upon with favor from the priests when he came to deliver the word from God. He was called to a hard and thankless job. Still, he remained faithful and God was faithful to him.

When our family was sitting in that special service with the African Children's Choir performing and the Jeremiah 29:11 was shared as the verse for a ministry that was being presented to the congregation I could feel God.

> *"For surely I know the plans I have for you, says the Lord, plans for your welfare and not for harm, to give you a future with hope."* Jeremiah 29:11 (NIV)

Going deeper in the verses of Jeremiah 29:12-14,

> *"Then when you call upon me and come and pray to me, I will hear you. When you search for me, you will find me, if you seek me with all your heart, I will let you find me, says the Lord, and I will restore your fortunes and gather you from all the nations and all the places where I have driven you, says the Lord, and I will bring you back to the place from which I sent you into exile."*

This letter in Jeremiah is to the exiles in Babylon. They were exiled by King Nebuchadnezzar from Jerusalem to Babylon. They were not in a good place and their release didn't look like any time soon; in fact it would be 70 years! Jeremiah tells them in the letter to be peaceful and obedient during this time and God promises to return them back to their home. The instructions are clear for them to search, pray and seek with all their heart. He is calling them to be faithful.

The individuals in the Old Testament tell us of God's faithfulness, speaking to us about our trust and obedience. Also, in the New Testament, Paul writes in 2 Corinthians,

> *"So we do not lose heart. Though our outer self is wasting away, our inner self is being renewed day by day. For this* **light momentary affliction** *is preparing for us an eternal weight of glory beyond all comparison,"* 2 Corinthians 4:16-17 (ESV)(emphasis added)

Paul's letter to Corinth speaks of his suffering and his amazing endurance. The joy that Paul had was the joy of being faithful, trusting and the acceptance of God's Will even when it doesn't seem to be reason to be very joyous.

We have afflictions in our life some are extreme and painful while others are light and temporary. It is in all afflictions that God is faithful and we are to trust and obey.

> *The steadfast love of the Lord never ceases, his mercies never come to an end, they are new every mornings; great is your faithfulness. "The Lord is my portion," says my soul, "therefore I will hope in him."* Lamentations 3:22-24 (ESV)

During this change in our life in both location, and distance from family and friends we felt close to God and a growing relationship with Him. There were times that we struggled with defining "home," then we came to acknowledge and gain comfort in that home was where the three of us were with God at the center. Many of us consider home a place of geography where we put down roots and stay. God is faithful and He shows us that our heavenly Father can reach us where ever we are in this world. We are to trust in His faithfulness and live in obedience to Him, our roots are in Him.

But blessed is the man who trusts in the Lord, whose confidence is in him. He will be like a tree planted by the water that sends out its roots by the stream. It does not fear when heat comes, and its leaves are always green; It has no worries in a year of drought it is not anxious, and it does not cease to bear fruit. Jeremiah 17:7-8 (NIV)

Talk Time

1. Define what life satisfaction for you is. What feels right that you don't want to change?

2. Look back over your life—what was good, what was changed that you didn't want to change and what would you choose to change?

3. In your life have you gone somewhere you hadn't planned on going? How did that work out for you?

4. *Jesus replied, "If anyone loves me, he will obey my teaching. My Father will love him, and we will come to him and make our home with him."* John 14:23 (NIV) What is your definition of home?

chapter

five

The Lesson

God provided and settled us in our life and in our definition of home in North Carolina.

The decision to relocate was hard from our everyday life. We left family, lifetime friends and a strong church home. There would always be times that we missed the comfort that in our life in Oklahoma had provided but, more important than all of that we embraced the comfort of our heavenly Father. God is faithful. He blesses us in ways we never considered or imagined for our life. We receive those blessings when we step out of our comfort zone. God is holding us up and transforming us.

If the Lord delights in a man's way, he makes his steps firm; though he may stumble, he will not fall, for the Lord upholds him with his hand.
Psalm 37:23-24 (NIV)

Mike had surgery to reduce his weight and our church family embraced and cared for us during his recovery. One of the best blessings during this time came on a day when we were in the house having a rough week. It seemed there was so much to do and with the limitations on Mike he was getting frustrated which led to me getting frustrated with everything. He looked out the window and panicked saying there was someone in our yard. I thought he was having hallucinations from the pain meds. So to appease him I went to look out the window. Sure enough there were two of the senior members of our church family out there taking care of our flower beds and shrubs. Tears come to me again even today as I share this story. I was overwhelmed as I went out to talk with them. The words were so hard to speak and yet so simple, "Thank you", "Thank you", "Thank you". We talked and laughed, she wanted to know if my weeds were rooted in China! Many blessings were poured out upon us during this time.

God was showing us love and teaching us to accept the gifts He provides.

There was an almost immediate improvement in Mike's health after the surgery. A local radio station had part time work for him and something else that began to take off for him was worship leading. He served a small local service at another church in our community and began to search for a worship leader position. Then our church began structuring for a contemporary service and Mike began serving as one of the guitar players for the service along with some worship leading. He also began praying with the intercessory prayer group each week at the church.

I continued to enjoy my position and the people that I worked with at the organization that had recruited me to North Carolina. In the church life I had begun facilitating Bible studies for women and became part of a Women's Ministry Team that started to organize events, studies and missions. A traditional fall women's retreat was organized as well as Bible studies in the fall and spring. I was blessed to be introduced to a wonderful woman of God named Angela Thomas. Her study, "A Beautiful Offering" and her message spoke directly to me. An opportunity to have her come to our church for a women's event had God all over it. Although many thought it would not be possible, God had other plans, over 200 women came to the event, and lives were changed.

An African mission team was also started and I went with a group to Kenya. It seemed that two of my passions in ministry were growing and I was able to share my love for them to others. The pruning was in action.

Makila had adjusted to school and church. The families with children her age became our extended family. We all had a passion for the children ministry at the church and our kids were at everything—VBS, Sunday school, Children's Choir, and any number of other activities. When Makila began participating in youth during the last couple of years in NC, she attended a youth rally where she accepted Christ as her personal Savior. God has richly blessed us with a beautiful girl, inside and out.

There was a sense of feeling "established" in North Carolina for us. A friend asked us how long we had been at the church and when we responded two years she laughed and said that it seemed we had been there longer. We made yearly trips to Oklahoma and we had family come to see us. I don't know that it felt it would be long term, but it felt stable.

Staying in the Old Testament;

> *Everything that was written in the past*
> *was written to teach us, so that through*
> *endurance and the encouragement*
> *of the Scriptures we might have hope.*
> Romans 15:4 (NIV)

Psalm 18; David praises our Lord, our rock, our fortress and our deliverer. This Psalm is one of thanksgiving written when David had been delivered from Saul. David became king and became established in his kingdom. He attributed it all to God.

Psalm 18:1-3 (NIV) we hear David's love and thanksgiving to God.

> *"I love you, O Lord, my strength. The*
> *Lord is my rock, my fortress and my*
> *deliverer; my God is my rock, in whom I*
> *take refuge. He is my shield and the horn*
> *of my salvation, my stronghold. I call to*
> *the Lord, who is worthy of praise, and I*
> *am saved from my enemies."*

Strength in the first verse is the Hebrew word for help, *hezeq.* Words used to define this include cure, repair and fortify. That is what this time was for me, Mike and Makila, God had repaired us, fortified us in

North Carolina. In reflecting, He may have fortified us more than we realized when we thought we needed repairing, He provided both for us.

Rock in this passage is a metaphor for protector; God is our protector, our stronghold.

David's life was filled with battles and being on the run from his enemies and from Saul. Saul did not like David and threatened many times to have him killed before his own death in 1 Samuel 31.

Dr. Henrietta Mears shares in her bible handbook the comparison of Saul and David's stature.

> "Both were kings of Israel. Both reigned about the same length of time, 40 years. Both had the loyal support of the people, and both had the promise of God's power to back them. Yet Saul was a failure and David was a success. Saul's name is a blot on Israel's history, and David's name is honored today both by Jew and Gentile." (6)

Why is there difference in their story, their mark on history? It is noted that both had the promise of God's power to back them. God was with them and placed them in their role as king of Israel. Saul's rise led to success which led to pride. He became insecure and a failure as king. He took his life when his sons were killed in 1 Samuel 31. David wasn't perfect but David had the heart of God. God placed Saul because he was after the heart of the children of Israel, the flesh and then He gave them David, a king after His heart, a heart for God.

There are many faces of David and his life can read like a good soap opera. He starts out as a shepherd boy, then musician, soldier, friend, outcast, betrayer, father, and most important a lover of God. Dr. Mears further describes David as a man after God's own heart not because of boasted perfection but because of confessed imperfections. 2 Samuel and Psalms gives us the roller coaster life of David. I would encourage you to dig deep into a study of the books of Psalm, Do it! I have been blessed to study online with Wendy Pope of Proverbs 31 Ministries in her ministry of Walking with Women Through the Word. I highly recommend her study on Psalms "Trusting God for a Better Tomorrow-A Study of Psalms".

When we study David we know that he loses his hold on God. He panics and when we panic the devil loves to get his hold on us. It is the decision of David to repent and come back to God that is the difference between him and Saul.

We need to stay connected to God; His way is perfect.

> *This God—his way is perfect; the promise of the Lord proves true; he is a shield for all who take refuge in him. For who is God except the Lord? And who is a rock besides our God?—Psalm 18:30-31 (ESV)*

A study of Psalm shows that David praises, gives thanksgiving and also boldly takes his frustrations and issues to God. There are times when we question and we wonder what is happening in our world, happening to us. This may make us question God, so ask him. Go to him with our questions.

This is where the story starts to change in our life in North Carolina. There were things that were starting to change. We were becoming frustrated and missing home again, desperately. I had some challenges with relationships at work and progress to make a difference in the organization. I felt a need to change jobs but chose to remain focused and drive the change needed in the organization; after all, I had a great team. The new contemporary service at church brought its share of frustration. A new concept of worship for a congregation with rich tradition is not easy to establish for a different way of worship. Events, both good and bad—were happening back home in Oklahoma and it was difficult and costly to make trips we wanted or needed to.

On November 19, 2012 the disruption in our lives occurred with my job. I was released effective immediately by the CEO. He struggled during the conversation to a point I had to ask if the change was immediate or would there be time to look for a new position, the release was immediate.

I could not talk with my team, close projects or box up the belongings in my office. A regular day turned into my last day by 9:30 that Monday morning, the week of Thanksgiving and the day after my husband's birthday.

I remember feeling the normal reactions of disbelief, anger and grief but I was given a peace when I walked in the door of our home and told Mike. I had already been looking at potential opportunities to return to Oklahoma and there was an interview scheduled, but I thought I would have time and could leave with a sense of accomplishment in my role. My phone rang all week, from board members, physicians and friends questioning and offering their support. Yet, my team with whom I had worked with and was quite close to was told not to talk to me.

I was shocked but also knew that God had brought us to North Carolina and He would take us on to the next place. One precious woman told us it was "God's next assignment" for us. We began to say that we were waiting on His next assignment and our prayers began to ask God for our next assignment.

As the job search heightened, we made the decision to drive to Oklahoma during the Christmas break in hopes of reconnecting and searching for jobs. The trip turned out to be about spending time with family. It was obvious that this is exactly what God wanted us to do.

Upon returning to North Carolina we put the house on the market in hopes of having it sold by spring break or summer. Then my friend Melissa called,,, it is always amazing how God puts her right in front of me when I need it. She talked to me about writing and telling of the glory in trusting God.

So here we are, the job change was decided for me and we were missing home strongly but Mike was growing in his ministry. He loved being in the praise band and rekindled his love for playing the guitar. Makila was in middle school, with its own set of disruptions in her young life.

Yet, there was a peace when all this was happening to us. It's O.K., I trust God to lead us and place us where He wants us. He knows our heart.

> *May he give you the desire of your heart*
> *and make all your plans succeed.*
> Psalm 20:4 (NIV)

> *May He grant you according to your*
> *heart's desire, and fulfill all your purpose.*
> Psalm 20:4 (NKJ)

In this waiting time we wondered what does God have planned for us?

> *He comes into our lives with ideals and*
> *truths which annoy and sting us and*
> *break up our rest, until He brings us to*
> *the one point, that it is only moral and*
> *spiritual relationships which last.*
> Notes on Isaiah, Oswald Chambers (7)

Joseph, Jeremiah, and David didn't have their lives uninterrupted once they reached a smooth path. They each remained faithful to God and each knew that God was faithful to them.

David shares with us his experience of honing in with God during times of wait, in Psalms,

I am still confident of this: I will see the goodness of the Lord in the land of the living. Wait for the Lord: be strong and take heart and wait for the Lord.
Psalm 27:13-14 (NIV)

Waiting has a purpose in our lives. God will use a period of waiting for us as well as for others to grow a deeper knowledge of God. It is not all about me, it's about God's higher purpose.

...God of all comfort, who comforts us in all our troubles, so that we can comfort those in any trouble with the comfort we ourselves have received from God.
2 Corinthians 1:3-4 (NIV)

God comes alongside us when we go through hard times, and before you know it, he brings us alongside someone else who is going through hard times so that we can be there for that person just as God was there for us.
2 Corinthians 1:4 (MSG)

Waiting is difficult when we use our own defenses, we are to open to God and let Him do His work during this time of wait. We will trust Him to take us and our situation for His glory.

Talk Time

1. *...Saul said, "When I saw that the people were scattered from me, and that you did not come within the days appointed, and that the Philistines gathered together at Michmash."...And Samuel said to Saul, "You have done foolishly: You have not kept the commandment of the Lord your God, which He commanded you. For now the Lord would have established your kingdom over Israel forever. But now your kingdom shall not continue. The Lord has sought for Himself a man after His own heart, and the Lord has commanded him to be commander over His people, because you have not kept what the Lord commanded you."* 1 Samuel 13:11,13-14 (NKJV)

    Commit your way to the Lord, Trust also in Him, and He shall bring it to pass. He shall bring forth your righteousness as the light. And your justice as the noonday. Psalm 37:5-6 (NKJV)

    The stories of Saul and David show us two leaders with different hearts, what are examples of those hearts in our world? Give examples of both—heart of the flesh and heart for God.

2. They both wandered from God the difference is one repented and returned the other didn't get back on the path. Do we wander? What causes us to wander?

3. *"my shield, and the horn of my salvation, my stronghold."* Psalm 18: 2b How do you apply that to your life?

chapter

six

Here We Go!!

*"In the future, when trial and difficulties await you, do not be fearful, whatever and whoever you may lose faith in, let not this faith slip from you—**God is Love**; whisper it not only to your heart in its hour of darkness, but live in the belief of it."*
The Love of God, Oswald Chambers
(emphasis added) (7)

NEWS FLASH!!! Waiting is not easy! Got that out of the way. Now we acknowledge that most of us struggle with the concept of waiting, we can move on.

My family is not different from yours. This time had its struggles but one thing that we keep in front of us is that God loves us and He will take care of us. We didn't know *how* or *when*, we just trusted He would, He has taken care of us many times before in our life and He would again.

During this wait we put our energy in church, Makila in school and me in a new job search. I spent a great deal of time completing incomplete projects such as cleaning and reorganizing the attic, closets, cabinets, garage and yard work. There was not a social agency in the county that didn't benefit from our reorganizing and some downsizing. Other projects included me reading and completing Bible study books in a basket I have collected over time. I returned to a passion I had many years ago in cross-stitching and crochet. The best is an afghan that I started in the mid 1990's, yes 1990's! I can't remember the year I started but I can now say it is completed along with many cross stitch patterns that I had saved but never started.

Makila has mom and dad home every afternoon and school work is the main topic in the house. Once during one of the study/review sessions she even asked when I was going back to work. I just smiled that momma smile. I realized how precious this time is even though she doesn't, yet.

Then this book started to develop in my mind, in notes, in my personal Bible studies. God was telling me something and I realized I could chose to ignore it or I could chose to move with it. I chose to move with it, though my pace wavered through the process.

Distractions came up along with fear and doubt as job interviews didn't develop into jobs and no one showed an interest in buying our house. The waiting grew longer and longer.

Mike and I both felt a call to ministry, Mike through his music and message and me writing and Women's Ministry. I struggled with how to get started and keep going with the writing. Then I discovered a conference that just so happens to be in North Carolina for women who are seeking to write, speak and/or lead women's ministry. I answered the call to attend "She Speaks" conference by Proverbs 31 Ministries. In preparing for the conference and looking at the topics and messages I knew there was something God had there to help both of us to become more established in the ministry God was calling each of us.

This event was in July, the middle of summer after I had been job searching for 7 months, the house had been on the market for 5 months and Makila was out of school for the summer. We planned to return to Oklahoma once again, in hopes of finding job opportunities. This was a busy summer, and the wait was getting longer.

I was diving into study in many ways. I would facilitate with my partner, Ginger at church, I was doing online studies, reading new books I had accumulated over time and with all of it I felt like a sponge. I don't know if I felt that the more I studied God would provide an answer sooner, or if I was trying to determine what I was missing in what He was teaching me. In the first of this book I shared I felt strong in my faith and that God was with me prior to our moving to North Carolina. It was just as true during this time even to a point that I didn't realize how much more my relationship with Him could be until this season in our life.

In my studies I found verse after verse in the Bible, and highlighted pages of books and devotional thoughts to share in this story. Yet that wasn't about the intent of my study, it was about me being in the word, reading and listening to what He had to say to me. This book is a reflection of that study and hunger for more of God's word and what He has for me. I have provided a list of studies at the end of this book. You will be blessed by the lessons you will learn. I want to share three key points.

- **Be in the Word**—in study with a group, devotions, individual reading, and study online. It is important to just be in the Word. He will speak to you, I promise. I used to do mainly devotions and they are great for a quick glimpse. The key is to be in a true study. With technology today you can do this in so many ways.

- **Pray**—pray in praise and thanksgiving, pray questions, pray fears, pray intercessory, pray out loud, pray for yourself,,,,,,,,PRAY! That is your conversation with God and He is listening.
- **Fellowship with Christian sisters and brothers**—we would not have survived as strong as we did in NC without our Christian sisters and brothers, our family. Melissa in Oklahoma and Ginger in NC are my sisters who push me, challenge me and let me vent. They also show me the verse and get me back on His path.

These three points have been consistent in most studies I have read. None of us can do this alone! We must be with God in His Word, in prayer with Him and be in fellowship with other Christians.

When I returned home from the "She Speaks," conference I was on fire and ready to get started on the ministry that Mike and I kept discussing with little action. We went to Oklahoma as planned and then upon our return to North Carolina, Makila started 7th grade.

The waiting was getting longer.

The job process was slow because of slow response or no response and there was no interest in our house. There were days of doubt and fear that sometimes led to melt downs. Mike and I can laugh because it seems the days he is up, I am down and the days I am up, he is down. Angela Thomas shared a story of those days when we feel Satan taking over our world. Shake your finger at him and tell Satan to get out of your house, get out of your situation, he does not belong there, God is in control. In our Sunday school class we shared the story many times. We all have those days and you have to tell Satan to GET OUT!

My big day was in September, we were almost a year in searching for a job and trying to determine what God wanted us to do. On that particular day Makila was sick and stayed home from school. Mike had gone to the store to get supplies for her recovery and I took the time to look at emails. A third job rejection in less than a week on jobs close to Oklahoma. I lost it, I was very frustrated and questioning God. It seemed that I was empty and losing faith. This was one of those days that Mike was up and I was down, down, down. There seemed to be so many doors closing and rejection with no clear direction or answers from God, my faith was floundering. Midafternoon the phone rang, guess who? Yep! Melissa! I melted down on her and you know what she did? She turned the table on me. She told me she couldn't wait to see what God has in store for me because what God is preparing is absolutely wonderful. I was reminded that my priorities are right, study and taking care of Makila. We hung up and I learned later that Melissa was not in her normal routine that day. She was taking a friend to an appointment and on her return home I kept popping into her mind,,,thank you God!!!

I was doing a study on praying at this time and on this particular day the question was about fear. Okay, no brainer.

> *Whether the fear in your life manifests itself as worry, doubt, insecurity, or timidity, know this: Jesus is in the door-closing business.* Prayers for a Woman's Soul, Julie Gillies (8)

> *When I am afraid, I put my trust in you.* Psalm 56:3 (ESV)

Through Melissa's encouragement, study and The Word I should be good for the day and with a peace covering me. Not on this day though, the attack is strong and I can't seem to keep the fear and doubt out of my mind. Mike and I talked and began to share our fears of running out of money. When that happens we wouldn't be able to go anywhere but the homeless shelter. The little savings we had wouldn't last long after the severance ended. I remind myself; the best choice is to give my fear to God and pray for wisdom and understanding. Faith helps me manage my life and the wisdom from God shows me the way.

> *If any of you lacks wisdom, he should ask God, who gives generously to all without finding fault, and it will be given to him.*
> James1:5 (NIV)

Later in the evening we were all watching TV. My mother called and I shared with her my day and the fears started coming back, the emptiness. She reminded me of the Peace and Comfort we have from the Holy Spirit.

Makila is feeling better and decides we need popcorn. I look at us, the three of us and our two dogs; this is what is important to me in my life. As I laid down that night I say my prayer knowing that God is my fortress, my strength, my comforter, my all,,,and I sleep.

I share all this with you in order to share the meltdowns not just the celebrations. God is with us in both—the meltdowns and celebrations. During this day I had had His Word, prayer, Melissa, Mom and Mike; not the whole arsenal, but pretty close and yet it took all day to fight the enemy. Discouragement is one of the enemy's strongest weapons and he will use it every chance he gets in the spiritual battle, he has had opportunity with us.

> *Two are better than one, because they have a good return for their work; If one falls down, his friend can help him up. But pity the man who falls and has no one to help him up! Also, if two lie down together, they will keep warm. But how can one keep warm alone? Though one may be overpowered, two can defend themselves. A cord of three strands is not quickly broken.* Ecclesiastes 4:9-12 (NIV)

The next day was better and a new energy came to me as I reignited the job search with new applications and 4 new recruiters contacting me. I spent time in the Word, two studies going at that time, and again, I prayed to God for wisdom and understanding in this trial.

In order to trust God, we must always view our adverse circumstances through the eyes of faith, not of sense. And just as the faith of salvation comes through hearing the message of the gospel, so the faith to trust God in adversity comes through the Word of God alone. It is only in the Scriptures that we find an adequate view of God's relationship to and involvement in our painful circumstances. It is only from the Scriptures, applied to our hearts by the Holy Spirit, that we receive the grace to trust God in adversity.

Trusting God Even When Life Hurts, Jerry Bridges (9)

A couple of weeks later I am no closer to finding a job and we are no closer to knowing if we are to relocate back to Oklahoma. I **am** closer in my relationship with God through my Savior Jesus Christ. I have been drowning myself in His Word and in study. It is as if I am a woman dying of thirst and God's word is my life preserver and thirst quencher all in one, the Spring of Eternal Life. Jerry Bridges book was very helpful to me during this time and I quote him again.

It is more than just knowing facts about God. It is coming into a deeper personal relationship with Him as a result of seeking Him in the midst of our personal pain and discovering Him to be trustworthy. It is only as we know God in this personal way that we come to trust Him. (9)

Something I have felt strongly about this time in my life and the life of my family is that God is not punishing us. It became clear to us that He was not yet ready for us to leave North Carolina at the time that we were ready to leave. Our involvement with the contemporary service at church, Makila with youth group, Bible study and starting a new Sunday school for adults seemed to all be part of God's plan for us before leaving North Carolina. We began to pray in agreement at our evening meal, that God knew our hearts, and our hearts wanted to return to Oklahoma.

Ginger had told me to watch a Charles Stanley message; she felt it was just for us. And, she was right. It was during his message that he shared a verse that he was taught as a young boy. This verse helped him through adversity and struggles. It is the words that the Lord spoke to Joshua giving him instruction after Moses is gone.

> *"Have I not commanded you? Be strong and courageous. Do not be terrified; do not be discouraged, for the Lord your God will be with you wherever you go."*
> Joshua 1:9 (NIV)

He gives us the same command today. When He tells us to be strong and courageous He is telling us to hold on and be alert. Joshua listened and obeyed the instructions that God had given to him and He brought him success. The success for Joshua was in taking the children of Israel into Canaan. Likewise, during our adversities, challenges and disruption we are to stay focused on God, listening and obeying His word.

The first time that Joshua heard these words from the Lord was through Moses,

> *The Lord himself goes before you and will be with you; he will never leave you nor forsake you. Do not be afraid; do not be discouraged.* Deuteronomy 31:8 (NIV)

God will repeat Himself so you get the message.

In holding on and diving into His Word I have said I felt like both a drowning woman and a woman dying of thirst. I have been searching for answers trying to find wisdom and understanding during this trial. It was as if I felt that my faith was lacking. I have learned that unanswered prayers or no prompt response from God does not mean my faith is lacking. It means that God has other plans, <u>better</u> plans for me and my family. We are to keep praying our prayers of burdens, unloading them onto Him. This is also a time of refinement for my faith. God refines us like silver and gold into the fire.

> *The third I will bring into the fire: I will refine them like silver and test them like gold. They will call on my name and I will answer them; I will say, 'They are my people,' and they will say, 'The Lord is our God.'* Zechariah 13:9 (NIV)

> *In this you greatly rejoice, though now for a little while, if need be, you have been grieved by various trials. That the genuineness of your faith, being much more precious than gold that perishes, though it is tested by fire, may be found to praise, honor, and glory at the revelation of Jesus Christ.* 1 Peter 1:6-7 (NKJ)

Our faith is refined by the various trials, fires and weakness along our journey. *Refine* is defined as purifying; to become free from impurities. That is why during the trials we are to go to our knees and not out the door. Our faith is on a continuous growth march and each step of the way God is with us pruning us, molding us to be stronger for Him.

God has been in all of this and continues to be in all of it. We have committed to ministry and have begun blogs and message posts while Mike has had special music and messages presentations. He has returned to song writing and continues to have a strong passion for praise worship leading. He has encouraged me to complete this book that I committed to God to write.

We have returned to Oklahoma after our house sold. We were able to close over the Christmas break so Makila could transition more easily to a new school—an answered prayer. We loaded up the U-Hauls and headed west after tearful good byes to our NC family. When the house sold we weren't real sure where we were going since we still did not have employment or even knowledge of possible employment. There was alot of anxiety and calls to God, as we prepared to move. One day Mike was in the garage working and I walked in to see him on the phone with tears in his eyes. His sister had called and one of their rent houses came available, the perfect place for us. Another answered prayer; a soft place to land as we looked at employment opportunities and Makila started school.

When we arrived in Oklahoma driving down the highway coming into town the water tower blazed the words "the Heart of Oklahoma," Remember our family prayer and that God knew our hearts and our hearts were in Oklahoma. He brought us to the heart of Oklahoma. He absolutely has a sense of humor!

Consider it pure joy, my brothers, whenever you face trials of many kinds, because you know that the testing of your faith develops perseverance. Perseverance must finish its work so that you may be mature and complete, not lacking anything. James 1:2-4 (NIV)

We each have times of challenges, afflictions, hurts, and disruptions that change the direction of our lives. It happens at any age, mine just happened to be in my late 40's, early 50's. Yours could be younger or older.

I love the line in the "Shake" song by Mercy Me, "No matter when it happened, at 7 or 95." We are all in the age range. The decision is ours, to turn away or accept Jesus Christ as your Savior. You may have accepted Christ many years ago and felt you had a stable faith then your choice is to go deeper in that relationship, He wants you to go deeper.

> *Let the morning bring me word of your unfailing love, for I have put my trust in you. Show me the way I should go, for to you I lift up my soul. Psalm 143:8 (NIV)*

Talk Time

1. *"Yet the Lord longs to be gracious to you; he rises to show you compassion. For the Lord is a God of justice. Blessed are all who wait for him!"* Isaiah 30:18 (NIV)

   What happens when you have to wait, on anything? This includes a food order, someone to come to meet you, a period in your life to move.

2. The three points--Be in the Word, Pray, and Fellowship, which one is the hardest and which one is the easiest? What do you do to make them all a part of your life?

3. *"For You, O God, have tested us; You have refined us as silver is refined. You brought us into the net; You laid affliction on our backs. You have caused men to ride over our heads; We went through fire and through water; But you brought us out to rich fulfillment."* Psalm 66:10-12 (NKJV)

   How do we "refine" our faith? God is with you in this refinement and you have an action to do in partner with Him, what is it?

4. What does going deeper in your relationship with God mean for you? How do you go deeper?

chapter

seven

Growing Through It

I want to share words of wisdom that were shared with me by a very special clergy woman during a crisis. The words are from JoAnn Miles who was the founder of the Women's Leadership Council for clergy women.

> *"I have never believed that God causes bad things in order to teach us lessons. But I do absolutely believe that with God's help the crisis in our lives can help us to become, more compassionate people."*

I would like to add that with God's help we grow closer to Him during our times of trials and crisis. We must choose to grow.

In writing this chapter, I would like to say that Mike and I have wonderful jobs and Makila has a scholarship to a college of her choice, but we don't. We do have answered prayers and peace in knowing that God has got it all in His hands and **that** is amazing success. He is providing to us every step of the way, we have not lacked with His provisions.

I have shared that I did a great deal of reading and studying during this time and there were many eye opening, mind opening and heart opening lessons that God taught me. The question from Melissa in 2008, "What did I learn?" stays with me today. The learning grew and became deeper in trusting God. The refinement is the refining of our relationship with God, a faithful God. Each step on our faith journey is a journey as He grows us closer, closer to Him. We are each where God is growing us and none of us are full grown.

Many times during the past year I have heard God saying to me, "I've got it." Sometimes with exclamation points sometimes I would listen and sometimes I would not. He still kept telling me, "He's got it," and He does! I **trust** Him!

In Paul's letter to Timothy in 2 Timothy he gives us this trustworthy saying:

> *For if we died with Him, we shall also live with Him.*
> *If we endure, we shall also reign with Him. If we deny Him, He also will deny us. If we are faithless, He **remains faithful**; He cannot deny Himself.* 2 Timothy 2:11-13 (NKJV) (emphasis added)

God remains faithful even when we are faithless. We have times when our faith is shaky and we struggle with trusting God. It may seem that we are faithful by going to church every Sunday, most Wednesday nights, participating or leading Bible studies, you know being the "church lady." Though we have been saved and acknowledge that we have accepted Jesus Christ as our Savior, have we really been at the table with Him? Do we get excited every time we open the Bible, His Word and read what His message for us? Is there a warm flush that comes across you each time you receive His message? Do I trust what Jesus can do for me more than what I can do for myself? Everyone has trials along their faith journey. It is the choice we make to trust, a choice to grow in faith and be faithful.

When we are in a time of being still and waiting, it is a struggle for many of us. Our first instinct is to resolve the situation ourselves, sort through the event and come up with our own answer. We react to the situation. When that doesn't go so well we connect ourselves to God. Our first instinct **should be** to connect with God first and only Him in every situation. Jerry Bridges tells us,

> *"Trust is not a passive state of mind. It is a vigorous act of the soul by which we choose to lay hold on the promises of God and cling to them despite the adversity that at times seeks to overwhelm us."* (9)

It was during this period of waiting that I realized what it meant to be thirsty, thirsty for the Lord. Then I asked for it, truly grasping His amazing Love for me and continue to grasp it every day. Celebrating each time I open my Bible and hear His message for the day. In our times of waiting we find trust, it becomes trustful waiting.

David is someone who talks about being thirsty. There were many trials, tribulations and you know lots of things that David endured during his life. We can read David's story in First and Second Samuel and in the Psalms we read David's words. In his words we see his thirst, love, devotion and trust of God.

> *My soul thirsts for God, for the living God.* Psalm 42:2 (NIV)

David was a thirsty man, he tells us in Psalm 42. We know that David lived in the dry desert which would cause the physical thirst for water but David tells of thirst for living water, a spiritual thirst. He was forced to leave his home and his place of worship. He can no longer hear the music, he longed for God's house and worship.

In Psalm 63, David was in the Desert of Judah. He is having an intimate conversation with God about his thirst and how he deeply searches for God using the geographic description, dry and weary land.

> *O God, you are my God, earnestly I seek you; my soul thirsts for you, my body longs for you, in a dry and weary land where there is no water.* Psalm 63:1 (NIV)

How do we have an intimate relationship with God? Do we get so busy in the business of our day, busy in our faith and not realize what we are missing? That is what I have come to know during my "desert time." This is not about geographical location it is about your location in your relationship with God, in your heart.

The time of waiting, being still and resting is a time to be with God. He calls us to rest, not to take a nap or a day off. He calls us to be still with Him, He has a plan. It is all about a process for us to grow in our relationship with Him and grow our faith in Him. God speaks to us, when we may not hear it, He will repeat.

> *One thing God has spoken, two things I have heard: that you, O God are **strong**, and that you, O Lord, are **loving**. Surely you will reward each person according to what he has done.* Psalm 62: 11-12 (NIV) (emphasis added)

He does keep repeating, we are always on a learning path and for some us that may have many lessons. You know, He won't give up on us. He is strong and He loves us. We need to plant our steps with God not our steps on the path.

One of my favorite things that I heard Beth Moore say at her conference was in regards to God's continual teaching in her life. He keeps on showing and teaching her and repeating to her. So much so that on her tombstone after the wonderful things about wife, mother and grandmother it will say "God got tired." I believe that would be said for all of us.

He instructs and we ask Him to instruct us. That may be difficult for us to ask because we are so overwhelmed with our circumstances. To trust Him we are to lean on Him for strength and guidance as He pours His love all over us. He lavishes us with His love. In the devotional

"Hope for Each Day," Billy Graham shares with us this thought:

> "*The Bible tells us that we only become stronger spiritually through exercise—through using our spiritual 'muscles' to meet the challenges of life. This is especially true when we face suffering and affliction, for they are one of God's ways to make us strong.*
>
> *Sometimes our God-given duty will include suffering. When it does, ask God to teach you through it.*" *(10)*
>
> "*Blessed is the man whom you instruct, O Lord.*" Psalm 94:12 (NKJV)

During this time I asked for instruction, teach me, show me, and grow me. He answered and I have a relationship with God that is stronger than my previous relationship and stronger than I ever thought I could be with Him. In conversations with God I have asked for wisdom and understanding of our situation, the wait and His plan. He blessed me with two women that I grew in reading and hearing their words. The first, Priscilla Shirer had a wonderful simulcast in April 2014 that as I listened I heard God speaking straight to me. In her message she shared the story of Elijah and his fortification through the process that God had for him, He has the same for us. We are to stay in the process and submit to what God has called us to and HE will sustain you, shelter you, surprise you and speak to you. There are blessings in the process and I can testify to that with a loud AMEN. Our blessings as a family and as individuals have overflowed our hearts beyond our minds.

The other woman of faith was an online bible study with Proverbs 31 Ministries teacher Wendy Blight with her book, "Living So That." A great study going deeper into God's word focusing on some of the "so that" verses in Scripture. She shares that God desires readiness and faithfulness.

> *"He starts with commands from His Word that require small steps of obedience. When we are faithful with these small steps, He will ask more of us. Each step calls us out of our comfort zones to go deeper still with Him, whether it be trusting in Him for salvation, trusting Him to honor His Word, trusting Him in prayer, trusting Him in a trial, or trusting Him to enable us to live our faith out loud for all to see."* (11)

What have I learned? First lesson, simply to say "I trust God" doesn't even begin to scoop the ice cream. What does scoop the ice cream? God wants a relationship with me that is bigger, deeper and better than I can imagine today or any day and add that cherry, I want the same thing!

When this book started it was about trusting God in this crazy world we live in, every day in every situation. What I have found is that trust grows when our faith grows. There are wonderful women of faith that we learn from and there are wonderful women of faith that we teach. Each woman of faith is a leader even though the work environment may be different, the positions we hold in an organization vary, and each family is unique. Our God is the same and He wants a relationship with you, deeper than you can ever imagine.

No matter what our trial He is with us every step of the way. No matter what, He is our **Joy** with us every step of the way.

> *But now, this is what the Lord says—*
> *he who created you, O Jacob, he who*
> *formed you, O Israel: "Fear not, for I have*
> *redeemed you; I have summoned you*
> *by name; you are mine. When you pass*
> *through waters, I will be with you; and*
> *when you pass through the rivers, they*
> *will not sweep over you. When you walk*
> *through the fire, you will not be burned;*
> *the flames will not set you ablaze. For I*
> *am the Lord, your God, the Holy One of*
> *Israel, your Savior;"* Isaiah 43:1-3 (NIV)

In book of Isaiah He tells us pretty clearly, He is with us today and He will be with us tomorrow in **all** things, we are His. He is faithful.

We will continue to be thirsty on our walk. It is knowing where to quench your thirst with His Water, filling us up to slosh out all around us.

So, what am I learning?

Three things, (1) God is strong, He is my strength, my refuge ;(2) He loves me and lavishes me with His love and (3) God is faithful.

Many are the woes of the wicked, but the Lord's unfailing love surrounds the man who trusts in him. Rejoice in the Lord and be glad, you righteous; sing, all you who are upright in heart!
Psalm 32:10-11 (NIV)

His pleasure is not in the strength of the horse, nor his delight in the legs of a man; the Lord delights in those who fear him, who put their hope in his unfailing love.
Psalm 147:10-11 (NIV)

Faith is the center, the core of who I am in Christ Jesus. When faith is center and you fill up and up and up with faith. And as you fill up with faith it crowds out doubt, fear, worry, and anxiousness because there is no room.

You cheer him with joy in Your presence.
Psalm 21:6b (HCSB)

Talk Time

1. Describe being thirsty? Differentiate body thirst versus soul thirst.

2. *My soul finds rest in God alone, my salvation comes from him. He alone is my rock and my salvation; he is my fortress, I will not be shaken.* Psalm 63:1-2 (NIV)

   What quenches your thirst? How?

3. What keeps you from a deeper relationship with your Lord and Savior Jesus Christ?

4. What did **you** learn?

Studies

Blight, Wendy, **Living So That**
Bridges, Jerry, **Trusting God**
Gillies, Julie, **Praying for a Woman's Soul**
Idleman, Kyle, **Not a Fan: Becoming a Completely Committed Follower of Jesus**
Lucado, Max, **You'll Get Through This**
Shirer, Priscilla, **One in a Million**
                                 Discerning the Voice of God
Smith, Hannah Whitall, **The God of All Comfort**
Swope, Renee, **Doubtful Heart**
Terkeurst, Lysa, **What Happens When Women Walk in Faith**
Thomas, Angela, **Do You Think I'm Beautiful**
                                 Joy
                                 Stronger

References

1. *Merriam-Webster.* (n.d.). Retrieved March 15, 2014, from http://www.merriam-webster.com/ dictionary.
2. Strong, J. (2007). *Stong's Exhaustive Concordance of the Bible.* Peabody, Massachusetts: Hendrickson. Note, that, unless otherwise indicated, the definitions of most or all Hebreww and Greek words in this book are from this source.
3. Halley, H. H. (2000). *Halley's Bible Handbook with the New International Version.* Grand Rapids, Michigan: Zondervan. 347-348.
4. Smith, H. W. (2010). *The God of All Comfort.* Amazon Digital: Public Domain. Location1072, pg 78.
5. Lucado, M. (2013). *You'll Get Through This.* Nashville, Tennessee: Thomas Nelson, pg 3 & 10 & 147.
6. Mears, D. H. (1999). *What the Bible is All About.* Ventrua, California: Regal. pg. 144.

7. Chambers, O. (2008). *Love A Holy Command.* Grand Rapids, Michigan: Discovery House Publishers. pg 74 & 40.

8. Gillies, J. (2013). *Prayer for a Woman's Soul.* Eugene, Oregon: Harvest House Publishers pg 35.

9. Bridges, J. (1988,2008). *Trusting God Evem When It Hurts.* Colorado Springs, Colorado: NavPress. pg 19 & 214

10. Graham, B. (2002). *Hope for Each Day.* Nashville, Tennessee: Thomas Nelson. pg 154.

11. Blight, W. (2014). *Living So That.* Nashville, Tennessee: Thomas Nelson. pg 253.

About the Author

Melinda Laird is a registered nurse and has been in nursing leadership for many years. She enjoys life in Oklahoma with her husband, Mike who she shares a passion for ministry. You can share in their ministry at blisscollective.org. They have a daughter who keeps them busy participating in her activities while in the fun "tween/teen" years.